HORSES SET I

CLYDESDALE HORSES

BreAnn Rumsch
ABDO Publishing Company

visit us at
www.abdopublishing.com

Published by ABDO Publishing Company, 8000 West 78th Street, Edina, Minnesota 55439. Copyright © 2011 by Abdo Consulting Group, Inc. International copyrights reserved in all countries. No part of this book may be reproduced in any form without written permission from the publisher. The Checkerboard Library™ is a trademark and logo of ABDO Publishing Company.

Printed in the United States of America, North Mankato, Minnesota.
042010
092010

 PRINTED ON RECYCLED PAPER

Cover Photo: Animals Animals
Interior Photos: Alamy pp. 7, 9; Animals Animals p. 19; AP Images p. 21;
    Corbis pp. 13, 15; Derek Middleton / FLPA / Minden Pictures p. 11;
    Getty Images p. 5; iStockphoto p. 17

Editor: Megan M. Gunderson
Art Direction & Cover Design: Neil Klinepier

Library of Congress Cataloging-in-Publication Data

Rumsch, BreAnn, 1981-
  Clydesdale horses / BreAnn Rumsch.
      p. cm. -- (Horses)
  Includes bibliographical references and index.
  ISBN 978-1-61613-419-8
  1. Clydesdale horse--Juvenile literature. I. Title.
  SF293.C65R86 2011
  636.1'5--dc22
                                        2010009358

CONTENTS

WHERE CLYDESDALES CAME FROM

Horses are graceful, powerful animals. For centuries, they have served as companions to people at work and at play.

These large mammals belong to the family **Equidae**. Their earliest ancestor was a much smaller animal called eohippus. This fox-sized creature lived about 60 million years ago. Since then, horses have developed into many **breeds**.

During the 1700s, Clydesdales were developed in Scotland for farming. They were named for the River Clyde near Lanarkshire. The Clydesdale was introduced in the United States in 1842.

Clydesdales were developed by farmers. Today, they are still useful in agriculture and forestry.

WHAT CLYDESDALES LOOK LIKE

Clydesdale horses are not dainty! They weigh from 1,600 to 2,200 pounds (725 to 1,000 kg). Clydesdales also stand between 16 and 18 hands high. Each hand equals four inches (10 cm). This measurement is taken from the ground up to the horse's **withers**.

To match its huge body, a Clydesdale has a long neck and a large head. The horse's face is flat and broad.

One of the Clydesdale's most recognizable features is its legs. Below the knees and **hocks**, the legs have feather. This long, white hair grows to the ground.

Under a Clydesdale's feather hide large, round hooves. When the horse walks, it lifts its hooves high off the ground. They are about twice as big as a standard racehorse's hooves! This size helps carry the horse's weight.

Most Clydesdale horseshoes measure about 20 inches (50 cm) across!

What Makes Clydesdales Special

Clydesdales belong to a group known as heavy horses. Originally, heavy horses were **bred** to carry knights in armor. Later, they were used as draft horses. Draft horses help plow land and haul heavy loads.

In the United States, most Clydesdales became city horses. Instead of plowing land, they drove carriages. They also performed in parades and competitions.

In the past, companies also used Clydesdale horses to pull wagons advertising their products.

This tradition continues. Today, Clydesdales are still used to drive the famous Anheuser-Busch wagon. For this reason, they are the best-known American draft horses.

Good qualities for a draft horse include strength, quickness, and calmness.

COLOR

Most Clydesdale horses are bay, chestnut, brown, or black in color. Clydesdales can also be roan. Roan horses have white hairs mixed in with one of the other colors.

Bay is the most common coat color for Clydesdales. Bay horses have light to dark reddish brown bodies with black points. Points are the horse's legs, mane, and tail.

A chestnut horse also has a brown coat. But it does not have black points. Brown horses have brown and black coat hairs with black points. Black horses have all black hairs.

A Clydesdale has white markings on its head and legs. A large strip usually runs down the center of its face. This is either a **bald face** or a **blaze**. Leg markings can be socks or stockings.

Some Clydesdale horses have white body markings. These are more common in Clydesdales than in other **breeds**. Clydesdales can have any mix of head, leg, and body markings.

A blaze marking (left) *is narrower than a bald face marking (right).*

CARE

In a stable, your Clydesdale needs its own stall. The horse should have plenty of clean bedding and fresh air.

A veterinarian should see your Clydesdale at least once a year. He or she can give **vaccines** and **deworm** the horse. The veterinarian can also float your horse's teeth as needed. Filing down any uneven teeth helps prevent chewing problems.

Clydesdale horses also need daily grooming to keep their skin clean and comfortable. First, remove any moisture with a sweat scraper. Then, use a rubber currycomb and stiff brushes to remove dirt. Finally, rub the horse with a grooming cloth to make its coat shine.

A Clydesdale horse's legs need special attention. The feather should be rinsed daily and washed with soap once a week. Don't forget to comb your horse's mane and tail to remove tangles.

Clean your Clydesdale's feet daily with a hoof pick to prevent discomfort. A farrier can trim hooves and replace shoes as needed.

FEEDING

Most Clydesdales are working horses, so their energy needs are great. Yet, horses cannot eat all the food they need at one time. That is why Clydesdales are usually fed three times a day.

Hay should make up the majority of a horse's diet. Types of hay include dried grass or alfalfa. Owners should also feed their horses grain. Common grains include oats, barley, and corn.

The amount of food needed depends on the horse's age and work. An adult Clydesdale may eat 25 to 50 pounds (11 to 23 kg) of hay per day. In addition, it will eat 2 to 10 pounds (1 to 5 kg) of grain.

Fresh, clean water should always be available. Horses can live only a few days without water. A hardworking Clydesdale can drink up to 30 gallons (115 L) of water per day!

In the wild, horses naturally graze on grass.

Things Clydesdales Need

Clydesdales are commonly used as driving horses. To pull heavy loads, they rely on driving equipment called tack.

A Clydesdale's tack has many parts, such as the bridle. This tack straps around the horse's head. It connects to a bit, which goes in the horse's mouth. The bit connects to the driving reins. The driver uses these long straps to control the horse.

A large collar fits around the horse's neck. Additional straps connect to this collar. They may run along the horse's body, behind the rear legs, and under the tail. Together, this tack is called a harness. It connects a horse to its load.

Horse harnesses should fit well. Each one weighs about 130 pounds (60 kg)!

A Clydesdale can pull some loads on its own. Heavier loads require a team of horses. Special tack connects the horses to one another. This helps them work together.

How Clydesdales Grow

A female adult horse is called a mare. A **breeding** male is called a stallion. After mating, mares are **pregnant** for about 11 months.

Clydesdale horses can be difficult to breed. Less than half of the mares become pregnant. Only some of them will have a healthy baby.

Baby Clydesdales are born live. A newborn horse is called a foal. A healthy Clydesdale foal weighs between 110 and 125 pounds (50 and 57 kg).

A foal will attempt to stand within its first hour of life. But, its legs cannot support its weight right away. This takes another hour or two.

Once the foal is standing, it begins to nurse. Clydesdale foals are **weaned** when they are about five months old. Most Clydesdales live about 20 years.

In the United States, about 600 Clydesdales are born each year.

TRAINING

Clydesdale horses can be trained for many uses. These include driving, riding, and competition. Training for driving begins at two years of age. A Clydesdale is introduced to the harness gradually. Then, it learns to drive a cart.

The Clydesdale can then be trained to work with a team. Teams are made up of pairs of horses. A new team member is paired with an experienced one. This teaches the new Clydesdale how to be part of a pair.

Each pair has a different role. The lead horses are **hitched** at the front of the team. The wheel horses are closest to the wagon. They are the strongest and do most of the pulling. Swing and body horses are hitched between these pairs.

Clydesdale horses are an amazing **breed**. They are huge, powerful animals. They are also beautiful and noble. It's no wonder these famous horses are known as gentle giants.

GLOSSARY

bald face - a white, wide marking covering most of an animal's face.

blaze - a usually white, broad stripe down the center of an animal's face.

breed - a group of animals sharing the same ancestors and appearance. A breeder is a person who raises animals. Raising animals is often called breeding them.

deworm - to rid of worms.

Equidae (EEK-wuh-dee) - the scientific name for the family of mammals that includes horses, zebras, and donkeys.

hitch - to attach an animal to a vehicle or an instrument.

hock - a joint in a hind leg of a four-legged animal. A hock is similar to a knee joint, except that it bends backward.

pregnant - having one or more babies growing within the body.

vaccine (vak-SEEN) - a shot given to prevent illness or disease.

wean - to accustom an animal to eating food other than its mother's milk.

withers - the highest part of a horse's or other animal's back.

WEB SITES

To learn more about Clydesdale horses, visit ABDO Publishing Company on the World Wide Web at **www.abdopublishing.com**. Web sites about Clydesdales are featured on our Book Links page. These links are routinely monitored and updated to provide the most current information available.

INDEX